Susan Butcher and the Iditarod Trail

This edition is published by special arrangement with Walker Publishing Company, Inc.

Grateful acknowledgment is made to Walker Publishing Company, Inc. for permission to reprint *Susan Butcher and the Iditarod Trail* by Ellen M. Dolan. Text copyright © 1993 by Ellen M. Dolan.

Printed in China

ISBN 10 0-15-365182-2
ISBN 13 978-0-15-365182-3

2 3 4 5 6 7 8 9 10   0940   17 16 14 13 12 11 10 09

Susan Butcher and the Iditarod Trail

ELLEN M. DOLAN

For my eldest daughter,
another special Susan

E. M. D.

Contents

ALASKA

Cartography by Ann Walsh

1

The Adventure

There was little snow in Anchorage in 1982, so the starting line for Alaska's annual Iditarod Trail Sled Dog Race had been moved north to Settler's Bay. Susan Butcher and her team, led by her Alaskan husky, Tekla, were an hour into the race. As they sped down a hill and around an abrupt turn, the sled skidded off the icy trail and crashed into a fallen tree trunk.

Susan's shoulder was bruised, and four of the dogs were jolted. They lost a little time reorganizing but were able to continue. Snow began to fall at dusk. In the dark Susan passed team after team until there were only three ahead of her. Although the trail had been cleared and marked with flags earlier, it disappeared under the deep snow. On the frozen Yentna River, Susan and the other mushers went from bank to bank trying to find a marker. Then one of the frontrunners found the trail, and Susan followed his tracks.

The trail went on and on, and Susan began to wonder why they had not yet reached the next checkpoint. Three of her dogs lost energy and began to limp. Susan put all three into her sled and continued at a slower pace. At dawn she met another musher coming back along the trail. He said they had all followed the wrong scent for ten miles and must backtrack to the original trail—a loss of twenty miles and several hours.

Not only Susan was discouraged; her team lost its keen desire to run. Dogs become bored when they re-trace a trail, and Susan's team was also pulling the extra weight of three teammates. She pushed on—talking to them, praising them. Early in the morning they reached the Skwentka checkpoint, only four hours behind her projected time.

Susan fed her dogs and settled them for a rest. Then she led her three limping dogs, Cracker, Ruff, and Screamer, to the holding pen. They would be flown back to Anchorage. After a good rest, the team revived and were on the move again. But forty-five miles along the trail at the next checkpoint, Finger Lake, Tekla, too, was limping.

Choking back tears, Susan untied Tekla and brought her to the holding area. Tekla, her first leader, had led the way on the first three Iditarods and had saved Susan's life on several occasions. Now she must be left behind. Tied securely to a tree, Tekla watched as her teammates pulled out of the checkpoint. There were eleven dogs left and almost 950 miles to go. More trou-ble lay ahead.

As the dogs began the climb to Rainy Pass, Susan's concentration wavered. She had had only a few hours' sleep since leaving Settler's Bay, and her heart was still back with Tekla. As the team neared the crest of a hill, Susan released her hold on the handlebar to help them to the top. She had not realized, however, how much power the dogs still had. Before she could catch the sled, they had crested the hill, raced down the other side, and disappeared up the trail.

Susan, her heart pumping with fear, ran after them. At each curve she expected to see a smashed sled and injured dogs. Her biggest fear was that the runaway sled would overtake them and crash into the team. Several miles down the trail she found them. The dogs were resting quietly, and the sled was on its side.

In spite of the team's joy at seeing her, Susan was tired, dispirited, and sad. She sat down to rest, but after a bit she shook herself up. A negative attitude would never win a race; she would think only winning thoughts from now on.

With stiffened resolve, Susan untangled the team and started off again. The dogs pulled steadily and they soon arrived at the Rohn checkpoint, where Susan had decided to make her mandatory twenty-four-hour stop. She fed the dogs and settled them comfortably for a rest. Then she lay down beside them in the snow to rub their shoulders, check their paws, and tell them how wonderful they were.

Rohn is the most popular checkpoint for a prolonged rest. Mushers have just finished the most difficult part of the trail, which rolls up and down on the way to a narrow mountain pass, then twists and plunges into an icy gorge. In the quiet forest at the Rohn stop, racers

Susan Butcher romps with one of her sled dogs. Owing to her unique bond with them, they develop great confidence and seem to think they can do anything she asks. SOURCE: PRO-VISION PET SPECIALTY ENTERPRISES

repair equipment, attend to their own bruises and cuts, and refresh their flagging spirits. After a day's rest their enthusiasm is rekindled, and they are eager to be on the trail again.

At dusk Susan and her team, well-fed and rested,

were ready to run again. They left Rohn and pushed into the Farewell Burn. The area near Farewell had once been covered with thick forest. Then in 1977 a roaring fire swept through the forest and left behind almost a hundred miles of blackened, rotting trees. Susan adjusted her headlamp and steered the team around hidden stumps.

Soon she caught up with the race leaders. A fresh snowfall had buried the trail, and they were waiting for morning to find it again. Susan joined them and took her turn at breaking trail. The run through the Burn and into the interior was long and tiring. When they reached the first checkpoint on the Yukon River, Susan rested again. She had a lighter sled stored and waiting there at the town of Ruby.

The snow had stopped falling when she left Ruby, but the temperature dropped far below zero. It was a long, cold ride to the coast and the town of Unalakleet. In the native language "Unalakleet" means "place where the east wind always blows," and the town rarely fails to fulfill this prophecy. A winter storm roared along the coast as Susan and her dogs battled their way from Unalakleet to the next village, Shaktoolik. Winds reached sixty miles an hour, and thirty-foot snowdrifts piled around the homes in Shaktoolik. Many of the dwellings were routinely anchored by chains driven twenty-five feet into the frozen ground.

For over two days Susan remained in Shaktoolik at the home of a hospitable villager. Even the dogs, who were bred for subzero temperatures, came inside. Susan chopped wood and tried to replenish her dwindling food supply from village fishermen. At last the winds began to diminish, and she set out again.

Fifty miles from Nome, the wind picked up again. By then Susan was traveling with the leaders: Rick Swenson, a two-time winner of the Iditarod; Emmitt Peters, also an earlier winner; and two other strong competitors, Jerry Austin and Ernest Baumgartner. She was in fifth place.

Several of her remaining dogs had raced along the coast before. Susan switched leaders, put an experienced dog in the front, and began to overtake the other mushers. She passed one, two, and then three of the racers. Rick Swenson was still ahead. Running, pedaling, willing strength into her team, Susan chased Rick all the way to the finish line. She crossed it just three and a half minutes behind him. She won second place and a $12,000 prize.

Over the years, the Iditarod Trail route has been changed slightly, and the rules for the race have been revised and improved. But the basic philosophy has remained the same. It emphasizes meticulous care of the dogs, stamina, and self-reliance. Racers do all the chores themselves, from harnessing their dogs and cooking their food to mending broken sleds and breaking trail. In their sleds they carry equipment required by the Trail Committee—snowshoes, an Arctic sleeping bag, a large ax, extra booties for protecting the dogs' feet, a day's supply of food for the driver and team, and promotional

Susan, dressed for the trail, wears warm clothing and a headlamp for visibility when driving on the trail at night. COURTESY JIM BROWN, IDITAROD TRAIL COMMITTEE

mail, or "cachet." (See photograph on page 8.) Most mushers carry more: a stove and fuel, pans for heating water and feeding dogs, treats for themselves, extra batteries for headlamps, spare sled runners, and tools. All are prepared to meet nature head-on.

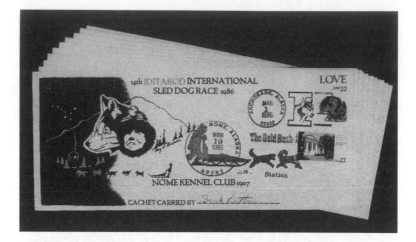

A stack of letters, or "cachet," is carried by each musher who enters the Iditarod—in recognition of faithful mail carriers on early trails. Each letter, which is stamped in Anchorage and again in Nome, after the race, is signed by the musher. The ones carried by winning mushers are auctioned at the Nome Awards Banquet to raise funds for the next race.
Source: IDITAROD TRAIL COMMITTEE

The thousand-mile trail begins in Anchorage and continues northeast to Nome. Twenty miles north of Anchorage is the first checkpoint, at Eagle River. Frequently the snow is sparse and the river ice soft here, so the dogs are loaded into trucks and travel several miles around open water to Wasilla, the race headquarters. Here the race restarts.

Outside Wasilla the trail runs directly into the wilderness. It leads mushers and dogs along a river, up and down the roller-coaster dips of Happy River ascent, up two thousand more feet through Rainy Pass and over the back of the highest mountain range in North America. The peak of Mount McKinley ("Denali" in the native tongue) can be seen only on a clear day.

The trail then curves down through the treacherous, icy Dalzell Gorge, runs on through the desolate Farewell Burn—country blackened by a massive forest fire—up the frozen Yukon River, out onto the pack ice and high winds of the western Alaskan coast, and on to Nome on the Bering Sea.

At the village of Ophir, shortly before the halfway point, the trail divides. In even-numbered years, it turns north to the village of Ruby and then south on the Yukon River. In odd-numbered years, it goes south through Iditarod and then north on the Yukon River. The two trails join at Kaltag. The alternate routes give more villagers in the interior of Alaska an opportunity to play host to the travelers.

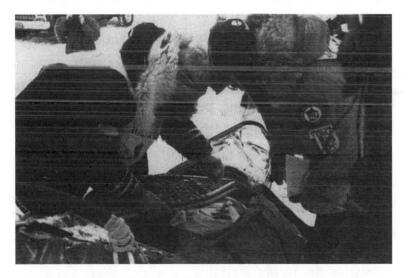

An Iditarod official checks for mandatory equipment. At each checkpoint the musher must show that an ax, snowshoes, dog booties, food, and other required survival items are packed in the sled. COURTESY JIM BROWN, IDITAROD TRAIL COMMITTEE

There are no roads to these isolated communities, and the Iditarod is the biggest holiday of the year. School is frequently closed, and children wait to greet the racing celebrities as they come through. Also waiting are huge pots of moose stew and plenty of coffee prepared by villagers for cold, hungry mushers. The Iditarod is not just a race. It is a way to put communities in touch with one another, a time to visit with old friends, and an opportunity to make new ones. The race, in fact, has become a symbol for the history and adventure of America's last frontier.

Along the trail there are usually twenty-six checkpoints. Many of these are in Athapascan Indian villages. Here racers sign in and show the checker that they have the required equipment in their sleds. Racers must take one twenty-four-hour rest at a stop of their choice and one eight-hour rest at White Mountain, the second-to-last checkpoint before the final sprint to Nome.

Racers cannot carry enough food in their sleds to last two weeks. So, long before the race, entrants fill burlap or plastic bags with extra food, supplies, and plenty of straw for the dogs. (The dogs are more comfortable resting on straw or spruce branches than on the frozen ground, and, on the average, they rest one and one-half hours for each hour running on the trail.) The straw and supply bags are flown into the checkpoints, ready for the racers' arrival.

Teams must have at least seven dogs—five of them in harness at one time—but not more than twenty. All these dogs should be of a northern breed, suitable for

An Iditarod racing dog enjoying a rest. The dogs in an Iditarod team get more sleep and attention than their owners. For every hour running, they rest approximately one and a half hours. Near the end of the race, a musher often gets just a few hours of sleep a day. COURTESY JIM BROWN, IDITAROD TRAIL COMMITTEE

performing in subzero temperatures. Although mushers may not add a dog to the team after the race starts, they may "drop," or leave, a tired or sick dog at a checkpoint. Volunteers care for the ailing dogs, which are flown either to Anchorage or to Nome for pickup after the race.

When mushers pull into a checkpoint, veterinari-

This careful musher checks his dogs' paws as the animals enjoy a rest. If necessary, he will remove bits of ice and smooth salve on the paws. Trail conditions will determine how often the dog booties are replaced (either on the trail or at the checkpoints). Icy trails cause the most wear.
COURTESY JIM BROWN, IDITAROD TRAIL COMMITTEE

ans are on hand to examine each dog to be sure it is still fit and able to race. A dog's health is always the top priority of both mushers and race officials. The vets provide salve for the dogs' feet and antibiotics when needed. And no matter how tired the musher may be, the dogs are the first to be fed.

In addition to a resident vet, each checkpoint has a volunteer ham radio operator on duty. Most of them supply their own equipment and frequently find that setting it up is a distinct challenge. In spite of electrical interference (possibly from the northern lights), they must be able to bounce beams along the trail so that there is constant communication between the checkpoints. They are the biggest part of the safety and information network on the trail. They know when each musher has left a checkpoint. If one is overdue at the next one, they summon help. One year an unconscious musher was found lying next to the trail. One racer stayed with the victim, another reported it to the "ham," and medical help was quickly on the way. In Alaska, people rely on one another.

It is this spirit that brings together a virtual army of other volunteers to help keep the race going. Pilots offer their time and planes to transport sick dogs, drop food bags, and shuttle a variety of officials and media people. The drivers of a fleet of "iron dogs," or snowmobiles, under the direction of a trail boss, post trail markers and clear trails.

Other volunteers answer telephones and record statistics. There is a race director, supported by the board and members of the Iditarod Trail Committee. The chief veterinarian has the last word on pulling a sick dog out of the race or disqualifying a racer who does not properly care for the dogs.

These individuals are at the heart of the Iditarod, a haunting name that conjures images of adventure, danger, mist-covered trails, wilderness, mountains, and encounters with the past. Even the route honors the past as it runs over a portion of a historic race in 1925 that saved the lives of countless people in Alaska.

2

Beginnings

In January, in the year 1925, the "Black Death" struck two children in Nome, a gold-rush town on the northwest coast of Alaska. "Black Death" was the northern name for diphtheria, a deadly disease. Its name alone terrified parents, for it was often young children who were infected. Symptoms of the disease were a sore throat and fever. These could quickly lead to rapid heartbeat, difficult breathing, choking, and soon . . . death.

Curtis Welch was the only doctor in Nome, but fortunately he was a good one. Dr. Welch had seen no signs of the "Black Death" for many years. Now he recognized its telltale white spots in the children's throats and knew it was back. Diphtheria spread quickly. More than fifteen hundred people, many of them children, were at risk.

In addition to the children, Dr. Welch was especially worried about the Indians in the town and nearby villages. They had not yet built up immunity to white people's diseases and would likely be the first ones to succumb to the infection. Except for trappers and fishermen, the natives had few disturbances in the North until 1898. Then their entire world changed.

In the late 1800s adventurers searching for oil accidentally found gold near Resurrection Creek in southern Alaska. Prospectors continued the search north and west and made several more strikes. Then in 1898 they discovered a bonanza of a field on the beach at Cape Nome.

Gold! Much gold! The word spread quickly, and thousands of hopeful adventurers raced to get a share of the prize. Almost thirty thousand prospectors arrived in Nome, set up a jumble of tents on the beach, and eventually mined $2 million in gold.

An early musher rests his dog team on Second Avenue in front of the U.S. Post Office in Nome, Alaska. In the early 1900s, teams like this brought mail and supplies once a month from Seward, an ice-free seaport in southern Alaska, to the gold-rush town of Nome. The U.S. Post Office retired its last sled-dog team in 1963. SOURCE: THE ANCHORAGE MUSEUM OF HISTORY AND ART

By 1925 the rush was over. Many of the successful miners had become worthy citizens, most of the disappointed prospectors had left, and the population of Nome was reduced to fifteen hundred. Nome became an orderly frontier town in place of a wild dangerous settlement filled with thieves and murderers. There were stout timber family houses on the side streets. And several main streets were lined with offices and shops offering supplies and services of all kinds: hardware, groceries, laundry, banking, lodging, barbers, lawyers, a post office, Town Council and Health Board offices, and a hospital.

The hospital was a large, two-story building, but Dr. Welch decided not to admit the diphtheria patients. He kept them isolated in their homes and treated them there one at a time. This would help contain the disease. But the only really effective way to stop an epidemic from spreading through the entire town was to vaccinate people against it. The doctor had a small amount of vaccine, or serum, but it was five years old—possibly useless—and would not go far. He must find more.

He went to the mayor, George Maynard, and the Town Council to ask for help. They recognized the emergency and immediately sent a wireless message to the territorial governor, Scott Bond, in Juneau. He in turn telegraphed requests for serum to hospitals and clinics in the Alaska Territory and the states.

At last doctors from a hospital in Anchorage, Alaska, almost one thousand miles southeast, answered. They found 300,000 units of the serum among their supplies. It was, however, the middle of winter in the frigid North. How should they ship the serum?

This was a difficult problem. There were three ways to get from Anchorage to Nome: by sea, by air, or by combined train/dogsled on land. Winter in Nome was so cold that the Bering Sea froze in rippling waves of ice. So no ship could get up the coast from Anchorage to Nome until the spring thaw. The second choice, by air, was risky. There were only two small single-engine biplanes near Fairbanks, Alaska, but they had been dismantled and stored for the winter. The third choice was a three-hundred-mile journey by train from Anchorage to Nenana, a town near Fairbanks, and then a six- or seven-hundred-mile sled-dog drive along a U.S. mail and supply route through the desolate, forbidding country in the Alaskan interior.

Many of the officials thought that one of the planes, reassembled, was the best answer. But it had an open cockpit, and its pilot had never flown at night or in January's subzero temperatures. If the plane iced up or crashed, both the pilot and the serum could be lost. On the other hand, it normally took almost a month to complete a dogsled journey from Nenana to Nome. It was a difficult choice.

Then the two sick children died in Nome and more were ill. The governor made his decision; it would be sled-dog teams on the land route. This trail through the mountains and tundra of the interior had once been used by Athapascan and Inuit peoples. Then the U.S. government marked, excavated, and maintained it as a route for mail and supplies to serve a network of gold-rush towns. The trail took its name from one of these towns, Iditarod. Along the route was a series of road-houses and cabins, each spaced about a day's journey from the next.

Governor Bond sent out an appeal for volunteers. He needed sturdy drivers and fast dogs. Members of the Northern Commission Company, which managed the trail, knew where to find them. Within two days, the plans were complete and the teams were in place. Some of the drivers and the dogs waited in the cabins and shelters along the trail. Many of these men were regular drivers on the mail route. The rest were all experienced mushers who either owned or borrowed strong dogs. They would relay the serum from musher to musher until it reached Nome.

The word "musher" is a corruption of the French-Canadian verb "marcher," meaning "to march" or "to go." In the early days, sled-dog drivers' word for their animals to move forward was "mush." "Musher" be-came part of the frontier vocabulary as the term for a person who drove sled dogs.

At the hospital in Anchorage on January 27, doc-tors carefully packed the vials of serum. They wrapped them in several layers of quilting and then canvas to protect them against breakage and cold. They included written instructions on how to warm the serum along the route. This compact, twenty-pound package could make the difference between life and death for children one thousand miles away. They rushed it to the train station, put it in the hands of conductor Frank Knight, and watched as Engine No. 66 pulled out.

As the serum traveled north from Anchorage, "Wild Bill" Shannon, an experienced musher, waited in Nenana with nine dogs. It was dark and very cold when the train arrived. "Wild Bill" took the package of serum, tied it to his sled, and called up his dogs. With a "hike" to the team and a swish of the sled runners, the serum was on its way across the Alaskan interior.

The next day Leonhard Seppala left Nome with twenty dogs and started south to meet the relay at a halfway point. His goal was the town of Nulato, 250 miles down the trail from Nome on the frozen Yukon River. Because of his fine reputation as a sled-dog racer, Seppala had been the first to be pressed into service by

Leonhard Seppala and his team of Siberian huskies. Born in Norway, Seppala came to Alaska seeking gold. He won every major sled-dog race in the North and was the first musher recruited for the task of bringing lifesaving serum to the citizens of Nome during a diphtheria epidemic.
SOURCE: ALASKA STATE LIBRARY; LOMEN BROTHERS COLLECTION

members of Nome's Health Board. At this time, he was
the most famous man in Alaska. Driving his fastest lead
dog, Togo, Seppala had won every important sled-dog
race in the North. Twelve-year-old Togo, a small Siberian
husky, was to be his leader again on this—the most
important race of all.

Meanwhile "Wild Bill" faced a number of problems. The temperature had dropped to fifty degrees below zero. Speed was important, but he could not push
his team too hard. The dogs' lungs might frost from
breathing heavily in the Arctic air. To protect his own
lungs, Bill breathed only through his nose. The bitter
wind howled and hurled snow in his face. The trail was
a blur.

Bill stopped once to rest the dogs and then quickly
moved on. Fifty-two miles out of Nenana, he reached
the first relay cabin. He was exhausted, but the serum
was still safely tucked in his sled. He gave it to the driver
waiting at Tolovana and then went inside to rest.

Musher after musher took the precious package.
They went over icy patches, up mountain slopes, down
into valleys. Most of the cabins were about thirty miles
apart. At many of them, the musher brought the serum
in to warm it before continuing. The relay went on
through the night into the day and the next night.

On January 29, Edgar Nollner waited in a dark
cabin at Whiskey Creek, close to the halfway point. Suddenly he sat up. Bells! Was he hearing things? He ran to
the window and found that it was Bill McCarty, who
had tied sleigh bells to his dogs, coming in from the

Ruby relay cabin. Mushers, either by choice or in some towns by law, often tied bells on their lead dogs to warn people they were coming up behind them. Edgar had not expected to hear Bill's bells for several days, but he wasted no time. He took the serum and started north along the frozen Yukon River.

The temperature was forty degrees below zero with a wind chill of sixty below. Edgar drove straight into the wind as the trail wound through desolate country. He brought the serum to his brother, George, at Galena, and George went on to Bishop Mountain.

After Bishop Mountain, the Yukon curves and turns south. The temperature continued to drop. It was sixty degrees below zero when Charlie Evans started his stretch of the relay. Before long, he noticed that two of his dogs were actually starting to freeze. He put them in the sled, covered them, and ran in front of the team himself to encourage the other dogs.

Charlie pulled into Nulato early in the morning of January 30. In less than three days, the relay teams had reached the halfway point. This was much faster than anyone had expected. Seppala was still traveling south from Nome. Instead of waiting for him to arrive and lose precious time, Tommy Patsy took the serum and went on north to the next stop.

That day the relay runners passed through three more villages. On the following day, January 31, Harry Invanoff left Shaktoolik and started north into a blizzard. For five miles he struggled through the wind.

Suddenly a team appeared out of the swirling

snow. It was Seppala. He was very surprised to see Harry—long before he expected to reach the relay. Seppala, Togo, and the team had already traveled 170 miles from Nome. But he knew, better than anyone, how urgent this relay was. His own young daughter had died

Leonhard Seppala, who became the honorary symbol for entrants in the Iditarod Trail Sled Dog Race. He moved from Alaska to New England and was the first to bring Siberian huskies to New Hampshire. His kindness toward his animals is honored each year when the Leonhard Seppala Humanitarian Award is given to the Iditarod musher who, according to race veterinarians, has taken the best care of his or her dogs on the trail. SOURCE: THE ANCHORAGE MUSEUM OF HISTORY AND ART

earlier from diphtheria. Seppala turned the team around and immediately started back to Nome.

Seppala had been leaving several dogs at stops along the way south so there would be a fresh team for the return trip. He would need them soon. Just north of Shaktoolik, the coast curves in around frozen Norton Bay. If he went along the shoreline, he would lose several hours, perhaps even a day. But if he cut across the pack ice on the frozen bay, it could break loose and carry them out to open water. There would be no way back. Seppala had great faith in his leader and was willing to stake his life on Togo's instincts. He decided to risk the bay.

The wind was fierce, often blowing the sled over and keeping the dogs at a slow trot. Togo went steadily on. The storm had swept much of the snow off the trail and exposed the glare ice below. The dogs frequently slipped and skidded sideways, endangering Seppala's grasp on the sled. The light began to fade. As night approached, it was only Togo's remarkable sense of direction and Seppala's determination that brought them across the bay and back onto the original trail.

Once safely on land, Seppala fed his dogs and rested for the night. It had been an exceptionally long run—over one hundred miles on the trail. As they slept, yesterday's trail broke off and floated out to sea.

The next morning Seppala prepared to start again, but could find no trace of a land trail. The wind continued to blow almost at hurricane force. Seppala could not even see the front of his team through this total "whiteout." It was Togo who felt beneath the snow, found the trail, and started for the next relay point.

In Nome more children were ill. Although Seppala did not know it, the Town Council had decided to send extra teams to help bring in the serum on its final run to Nome. Three more teams driven by Charlie Olson, Ed Rohn, and Gunnar Kaasen left Nome. They were to space themselves in cabins along the last eighty miles of coastline.

Seppala and his team were battered and exhausted when they reached Olson, who was waiting at Golovin. Togo had led the teams all the way — 250 miles. Olson transferred the serum, went out into fifty-mile-per-hour winds, and battled his way through treacherous weather for another twenty-five miles. At Bluff he passed the serum to Kaasen, who was to bring it on to Ed Rohn.

At the head of Kaasen's team was a handsome black dog, Balto. He was not as fast as Togo, but he was strong and steady. Although Seppala used Balto to haul freight, he did not choose him for his relay team. Kaasen had always thought Balto was a brave dog. He would be proved right.

The wind was still roaring when Kaasen and the team started out. Snow piled in drifts around the dogs and covered them up to their stomachs in places. Balto pulled with all his strength and the rest of the team followed. The sled moved forward haltingly. Balto had found the trail again, and the relay continued.

Then, abruptly, Balto stopped. Kaasen shouted at him to go on, but the dog would not move. Kaasen ran

25

forward to see what was wrong. Balto was standing in several inches of icy water. They were on the bank of the Topkop River, and the ice below was beginning to give way. Had they continued, the team and sled would have pitched forward into the river. Balto knew what he was doing. As soon as Kaasen dried the dog's feet, Balto made a turn and led the team around the river and back to the trail.

Once during the trip the sled overturned and the serum flew through the air. Blinded by the whirling snow, Kaasen could not find it. He grew frantic as he searched. Had it come all this way, just to be lost on the final fifty miles?

Desperately he felt around. It had to be somewhere in the snow. The dogs watched curiously as Kaasen yanked off his gloves, got down on his knees, and dug in the snow. He was afraid to move too far from the sled and lose his sense of direction. At last his hand closed on the package. This time he tied it very tightly to his sled. Balto moved on.

When they reached Port Safety, where Rohn was waiting, Kaasen did not see the light that usually signaled that a musher was inside. The storm had destroyed all of Nome's telegraph communications, so Kaasen did not know that the Town Council had called a temporary halt to the relay. Kaasen was not sure what to do—stop or go on. At last he decided that even if Rohn was inside, he must be asleep. It would take him precious time to dress and harness his dogs. Balto and the team were going well, the weather was improving, and Nome was now twenty-five miles away. Kaasen decided to keep going.

Just after dawn on February 2, Balto led the final relay team into Nome. The dogs and Kaasen were half-frozen and bone tired. At 5:30 A.M. Kaasen knocked on Dr. Welch's door. When the doctor, thinking someone else was ill, answered it, he was astonished. It had taken just five days, seven and a half hours to complete a journey that usually took at least twenty-five days.

The doctor got busy. With a good supply of fresh serum, he was able to continue vaccinations. From then on, there were no new cases of diphtheria. Within three weeks, the quarantine was lifted and the people of Nome were safe again.

This dramatic rescue caught the attention of the entire country, and mushers and their dogs became instant heroes. Medals, citations, and other rewards were heaped on the courageous men. Seppala, who was the best-known of the mushers, later moved to New England and continued to race his sled dogs for many years. Togo, somewhat lamed by the long relay, remained his favorite leader until he was retired at sixteen years of age. Seppala, who raced for over forty-five years and traveled an estimated 250,000 miles by dog team, was the first to introduce the Siberian husky breed to the "lower forty-eight" states. In 1966 when the Dog Mushers' Hall of Fame was built near Knik, Alaska, Seppala and Togo were among the first chosen as members.

Kaasen and Balto, who made the final run into Nome, received $1,000 from the company that pro-

A bronze statue of Balto, an almost totally black sled dog, stands in New York's Central Park as a tribute to all sled dogs who ran the relay of almost seven hundred miles across Alaska from Nenana to Nome in 1925. Frederick G. R. Ross, the sculptor, won the National Academy Design Award for his work on the 1925 statue. SOURCE: PARKS PHOTO ARCHIVES, CENTRAL PARK

duced the serum plus movie offers and newspaper coverage around the world. Later that same year a bronze statue of Balto was placed in Central Park in New York City. It is still there. Children can sit astride his bronze back, pat his sides, and imagine a snow-covered trail in the distance.

A plaque under the statue says, "Dedicated to the indomitable spirit of the sled dogs that relayed antitoxin six hundred miles . . ." At the base of the statue is a salute to all brave sled dogs: "Endurance-fidelity-intelligence."

3

The Iditarod Trail

In the early days of Alaska, sled dogs were necessary for transportation and hunting. Nearly every family in an Eskimo village had its own team, and the dogs were frequently pets as well as working animals. Descended from wolves, the dogs grew a rough, shaggy outer layer of fur and a thick waterproof undercoat that enabled them to survive in subzero temperatures. Their feet were snowshoe-flat and cushioned with fur for protection because the teams traveled in deep snow and over shards of ice.

By the 1900s Alaskan malamutes, northern Eskimo dogs, were common in Nome. They were large, powerful dogs used for hauling freight. In 1910, Siberian huskies, faster, smaller, and lighter than the malamutes, were imported from Russia. It wasn't long before dog owners began to boast about their teams' speed. To stir up a little excitement during long winter months, the mushers in Nome decided to test which one had the fastest team.

Scotty Allan, whose young son, George, had orga-

Winners of the first annual All-Alaska Sweepstakes in 1908 in Nome.
The team was driven by John Hegness for its owner, Albert Fink, one of
the organizers of the race. Scotty Allan, the other organizer, and
Leonhard Seppala were winners in subsequent years. It was the first
organized sled-dog race in North America recorded by the International
Dog Racing Association. The teams ran a four-hundred-mile race in just
five days. SOURCE: ALASKA STATE LIBRARY; LOMEN BROTHERS COLLECTION

nized and won a sled-dog race for schoolboys, joined
Albert Fink, a Nome lawyer, and formed a kennel club.
Its purpose was to improve and record the current dog
breeds and try to make conditions better for the animals. In 1908 the club held the first official sled-dog
race in America, the All-Alaska Sweepstakes.

This race was a four-hundred-mile round-trip
from Nome north along a telegraph line to the village of
Candle on Kotzebue Sound. Nearly everybody in Nome
gathered at the starting line to see ten teams leave one
at a time. They waited nearby for telegraphed reports
on the progress of the race. The contest was an instant
success, and the Sweepstakes became an annual event
until the beginning of World War I.

Forty years later, Joe Redington, a young man who would make Alaskan sled-dog racing famous throughout the sports world, arrived in the North. Joe's adventures began on the famous Chisholm Trail in Oklahoma, where he was born. His mother abandoned the family shortly after his birth. Joe's father was a laborer who moved from ranch to farm to mine as a job opportunity arose. Joe and his brother went with him, and in 1948, the three drifted to Alaska.

Joe liked what he found there. With part of his slim funds, he bought land in the town of Knik, north of Anchorage and near a stretch of the abandoned Iditarod Trail. He immediately became fascinated by sled-dog racing, began to buy dogs, and, within a year, established a breeding kennel of his own.

For several years Joe used his dogs to earn a living (hauling timber or doing rescue work) and for fun (racing). This method of living so suited him that he became dismayed when he saw the sled dogs he loved slowly being replaced by machinery. By 1960, snowmobiles and all terrain vehicles (ATVs) did the work of sled dogs in many villages. These dogs were part of the life-style and history of Alaska. Joe did not want to see the breeds disappear.

Then he found a way to do something about it. In 1966 he met Dorothy Page at a winter carnival in nearby Wasilla, Alaska. Dorothy, transplanted from California, was a gifted organizer who also loved history. The 100th anniversary of the the U.S. purchase of the Alaska Territory from Russia was to be celebrated in 1967. Dorothy was president of the local centennial committee and wanted to celebrate with an event both historical and exciting. Joe had just the answer for her—a sled-dog race. Dorothy, who loved the sled dogs as much as Joe, decided a race would be an excellent event. And if enough of the nearby Iditarod Trail could be restored, it would be a special tribute to Alaska's history.

In February 1967, the opening ceremonies were held for the centennial race, which was run in two heats over a twenty-five-mile portion of the old Iditarod Trail. Leonhard Seppala, who was such a key figure in the serum run, was chosen as an honorary representative of all competing mushers. He was coming from the East to participate, but shortly before the race started he died. His wife, however, came to the ceremonies and scattered his ashes over part of the trail. Alaskans thought it the best possible resting place for one of their mushing heroes.

The relatively short "sprint" race was an unexpected success. More than fifty racers entered, and Isaac Okleasik of Teller, Alaska, won the $7,000 first prize. This encouraged Joe to try for more. He wanted to raise money for a larger prize, and he wanted a long-distance race covering the six hundred miles from Knik to the village of Iditarod, namesake of the trail. He soon encountered questions, however, from new residents.

"What's Iditarod?" they asked.

"Where in the world is Iditarod?"

Iditarod is a ghost town deep in the Alaskan interior. Its name comes from "Haiditarod," the native word meaning a "far, distant place." To early Indians, this spot was far from regular fishing places and distant from any shore.

Then in 1908 on Christmas Day, two prospectors discovered gold in Otter Creek and started the last major Alaskan gold rush. The prospectors had intended to keep the news of their find quiet, but word leaked out and within a year thousands of hopeful miners from other crowded or waning goldfields arrived. Newcomers dropped the native "H" and the "a," called the spot "Iditarod," and quickly made it a boomtown. In a short time there were several hotels, cafés, saloons, stores of all kinds, family-owned boardinghouses, cabins, tents, homes, and ten thousand people in the settlement.

This boom helped to further develop the trail serv-

A scene on First Avenue in the busy gold-rush town of Iditarod in the 1900s. Shortly after this photograph was taken, a fire destroyed many of the buildings. They were rebuilt, and the town flourished until the nearby goldfield played out. Now a ghost town, Iditarod is the halfway stop every other year on the southern leg of the Iditarod Trail Sled Dog Race.
SOURCE: ALASKA STATE LIBRARY; BASIL C. CLEMONS COLLECTION

ing the interior. Once a month mail from the ice-free city of Seward came in and a supply of gold went out. In good weather travelers walked, rode bicycles, and drove horses as well as dogs along the trail.

Iditarod was still a three-week trail ride to Anchorage. Townspeople created their own fun with hayrides, dances, skiing on old barrel staves, an occasional visit from a traveling clergyman, and the newest pastime: sled-dog racing. In 1911 Joe Jean of Iditarod brought fame to his town when he took a strong dog team to Ruby, raced in a local Sweepstakes-style competition, and won that sprint race in less than sixty hours.

By 1914 the gold was gone and so were most of

A musher encourages his team as they race through the town of Ruby, Alaska, in the early 1900s. Sprint races, drawing the best teams from each village, were a popular activity during the long, isolated winter months in the Alaskan interior. Ruby later became a major stop on the Iditarod Trail Sled Dog Race. SOURCE: THE ANCHORAGE MUSEUM OF ART AND HISTORY the people. Today Iditarod is a place of abandoned, crumbling buildings. Shutters bang and door frames sag on the old structures. A rusting vault still stands in the former bank building, but it no longer holds gold, only the dust of memories.

So it wasn't surprising that young Alaskans did not know much about Iditarod. Joe Redington adjusted his sights and decided to plan a race that would go through Iditarod, and then all the way to Nome. Surely everyone knew where Nome was. But many predicted that an effort to race more than one thousand miles across the country was impossible. Joe paid no attention to them and dreamed on.

During winter mancuvers the U.S. Army cleared a large portion of trail. Joe and Dorothy worked to plan a route and set guidelines and rules for the race. Joe promised a purse of $50,000 to be shared among the top winners, even though he was not sure he could raise that amount. Volunteers offered help and money to make Joe and Dorothy's unlikely dream become a reality.

The Iditarod Trail Sled Dog Race was first held in 1973 and is, to this day, considered the toughest race in the world. Because the race is more than one thousand miles and because Alaska is the forty-ninth state to be admitted to the Union, Joe billed the official mileage as 1,049. Actually it is somewhat longer and varies from year to year according to trail conditions.

In that first race there were thirty-four entrants, a purse of $50,000, and a first prize of $12,000. The winner was Dick Wilmuth, who raced from Anchorage to Nome in twenty days. By the time of the twentieth Iditarod race in 1992, there were seventy-eight entrants, a purse of $300,000, and a first prize of $50,000. It was won by Swiss-born Martin Buser of Big Lake, Alaska, who made it to Nome in a record ten and four-fifths days.

The first week of March each year focuses national media attention on the bustling city of Anchorage. The whole world watches as this impossible, imaginative adventure begins.

At the beginning of the 1987 Iditarod race, the holding pen near Fourth Avenue in Anchorage was filled with dog trailers, mushers, helpers, handlers, sleds, children, and hundreds of barking dogs. Racers checked supplies for the last time and repacked their sleds. Unwary spectators tripped over the trailing wires of media equipment. All had the air of expectancy found before a big party.

By 8:30 A.M. mushers began to tie on white vests displaying their race number, drawn at a banquet two nights before. Veterinarians, who had examined every single dog for health and fitness during the previous week, helped officials mark each animal with a dab of paint to prevent an exchange during the race. Some of the dogs, who tried to quick-dry the mark by shaking their heads, scattered paint on nearby spectators.

The first dozen racers left the pen and began to line up along Fourth Avenue, ready to leave at two-minute intervals. Picket snow fences lined both sides of the street for several blocks, keeping back spectators and forming a two-lane path, or "chute," for the start.

Most of the racers found this the most difficult time in the entire race—far worse than running on an icy mountain trail. The dogs, accustomed to living and training in the wilderness, were distracted by the big city bustle: noise, confusion, tall buildings, stoplights, police whistles, flashing cameras, and loudspeakers.

The well-rested dogs were in top condition, filled with energy, and in a frenzy to move. They strained at their harnesses, leaped in the air, jumped sideways over their hitches, frantic to be on their way. There could be no question that these animals were born to run. Standing beside each dog and grasping its harness was a handler, feet dug in and body leaning backward at a forty-five-degree angle.

A second sled, guided by a friend or relative, was attached behind each musher's sled. The extra weight helped slow the first rush of the powerful animals, and the extra person was there to help if trouble arose in the first few miles of the race. When the racer reached the first checkpoint at Eagle River, the auxiliary sled would be dropped.

Just before 9:00 A.M. race officials moved ceremoniously toward the starting line. Spectators were momentarily subdued and quiet. All was ready. The race marshal cut the ribbon.

"Number one!" she called.

No one moved. This spot was always honorary. For

many years it was reserved for Leonhard Seppala and later for other serum mushers and dignitaries.

After two minutes of respectful silence, the race marshal raised her head and looked down the line of sleds. The first mushers were in position.

"Number two!" she called. ". . . five, four, three, two, one, go-ooooo!"

The handlers released the dogs and jumped back.

"All right!" called the first musher.

Out of the chute came an eager team of dogs driven by a determined young woman, Susan Butcher. This year she would run one of the most exciting races in Iditarod history.

4

Susan Goes Coast to Coast

Susan Butcher was born on December 26, 1954, in Cambridge, Massachusetts, a college town near Boston. Her parents, Charlie and Agnes Butcher, were progressive thinkers who encouraged Susan and her sister, Kate, one year older, to be independent. Charlie, the head of the family's chemical products company, shared an enthusiasm for boats and sailing with his daughters. Agnes, a psychiatric social worker, firmly believed that her children should not be forced into a parental mold, but rather allowed to develop their own special qualities.

From early childhood Susan loved animals and the outdoors. A rainstorm was not something to avoid; it was to be enjoyed, splashing through puddles and soaked to the skin. A dog was not just a pet; it was a friend, asking only for affection. Susan was four years old when she got her first dog. Cabee, part Labrador retriever, soon became the most important thing in her life.

Susan's preference for space and freedom was documented early. When she was eight, she wrote a paper for school declaring "I Hate the City." She had a better grasp on this theme by fourth grade, when she wrote "I hate the city because society is ruining things for the animals. . . ."

Animals were always a priority with Susan. Three times a day she took Cabee for exercise. As they walked through the streets, she called up other neighborhood dogs to join them. Soon she was traveling with a pack of fifteen to twenty dogs. Watching and listening, Susan began to learn how dogs communicate. She soon knew by a bark or howl which dog was in a bad mood, which one was feeling playful, which one was timid or afraid. These special times each day became the groundwork for her later impressive success in training and racing dogs.

By the time Susan was in junior high school near Cambridge, the administrators discovered that she had mild dyslexia. A tutor helped her with her English classes. Dyslexia has nothing to do with intelligence, rather with the processing of written words and sometimes numbers. Letters and numbers are often transposed or reversed—the reader may see "top" instead of "pot" or "31" instead of "13" or "b" for "d." The eye may skip over a letter and see "ws" for "was." And next time, the text could look completely different.

Dyslexic students are frequently labeled "lazy" or "stupid" when, in fact, they are struggling with all their might to read a passage that looks like total nonsense. A classmate may fluently read aloud, "On Friday the 13th, a witch stirred a magic brew in her black pot." The dyslexic may see "On Frbay the 31th a wtch strrb a magc drw in hr dlck top."

Sometimes with very bright students, the problem is not identified until late, and the dyslexic often compensates or displays remarkable ability in areas other than English. Susan's flow of verbal English was excellent, and she scored high in mathematics and science. She was also a "natural" in sports. With zest and much skill, she played through the seasons. There was field hockey in the fall, basketball in the winter, softball in the spring, and swimming in the summer. She was especially able and confident at sailing, taking risks that made even the older boys gasp.

Sailing was an important part of Susan's vacations at the family's summer home on the coast of Maine. She spent many happy hours on the beach at Brooklin, just west of Bar Harbor. In this area, shipbuilding has been a major industry for generations and hard work a way of life. Charlie taught Susan and Kate to sail and bought each of them a set of professional tools used for shipbuilding. They spent two seasons trying to rebuild an old sailboat.

Although they never succeeded in making it seaworthy, the activity satisfied Susan's desire to be away from people. On the beach the stifling effect of Cambridge dissolved as she enjoyed the freedom of the sky, the sea, the endless shore. Over and over she looked at the distant horizon, dreamed of building a wooden boat and sailing around the world—alone.

Before Susan was out of high school, her parents

A stretch of the coast of Maine, near the beach where Susan Butcher spent many summer vacations. Susan was a skilled sailor, and her earliest ambition was to build her own boat and sail into the horizon — alone.
SOURCE: THE LIBRARY OF CONGRESS

divorced. Charlie moved to Colorado and remarried. When she was fifteen, Cabee died. It was a difficult time. Then her aunt sparked a new interest when she gave Susan another dog, a Siberian husky named Maganak. This was the breed Leonhard Seppala had raced and first introduced to New England. Susan was pleased with her new pet and especially with the history of huskies as sled dogs.

Out of curiosity she began to attend sled-dog races in nearby New Hampshire. She was so intrigued that she went to the library, searched for books on sled dogs, and began to train Maganak. She went to more races. Then she bought another husky, a teammate for Maganak.

But that proved to be one too many for Susan's mother. Agnes did not want two large dogs in her house. Susan was sincerely attached to her pets, so she and the dogs went north to her grandmother's home in Maine, where she finished high school. Susan continued to maintain a warm relationship with her mother.

Because of her parents' attitude, Susan grew up believing that being a female did not limit her goals. But when she applied for admission to a boat-building school in Maine, she was refused, obviously because she was a woman. Before she was even out of her teens, Susan had to deal with the frustration of dyslexia, the upheaval of her parents' divorce, the death of a favorite pet, and the unfairness of sexual discrimination.

The confidence and independence built through the years served her well at this important juncture in her life. It was time for another step forward. With her love for animals and her interest in sled-dog racing pulling her, Susan set her sights on Colorado. She knew there was a sled-dog community near Denver and also that Charlie would be close by. Kate, who had also come north to Maine, became a professional carpenter there, and Agnes later moved to Maine as well.

In 1972, when she was seventeen years old, Susan left the coast of Maine for the mountains of Colorado. When she arrived in Boulder with her two dogs, there was a surprise waiting. Her stepmother had ordered a dogsled for her from a racing kennel. They went to pick it up, and Susan met the woman who owned the kennel. Within a short time, Susan bargained her way into a job there. She would help train and run the dogs, and the owner would provide her room and board.

In addition to her own dogs, Susan had fifty others to train and race. She also registered at nearby Colorado State University for veterinary classes and was later hired as assistant to a veterinarian. She learned how to give shots, take temperatures, check heartbeats, locate fractures, and ease pain for a large variety of animals. Susan's parents had often thought that she would become a veterinarian because of her love for all animals. But Susan soon realized that this future would mean spending most of her days in an office. That was not at all what she wanted.

As she was paging through a magazine one day, she saw an article about the first running of the Iditarod race in Alaska. It had an immediate impact. In Colorado a racer hangs on to the back of the sled and enjoys the ride. In Alaska the musher pumps with one foot, runs up hills, and actively helps the dogs. Susan liked the Iditarod's tough, bare-bones approach to racing; it seemed to echo her own attitude. She preferred work to play, and Alaska offered a life-style where hard work would be the mark of success. During her stay in Colorado, one of her dogs was stolen and the other killed by an automobile. In 1975 Susan went north to the last frontier, Alaska.

Her first job there was in Fairbanks. The University of Alaska ran a program to save the endangered musk-ox, and Susan, experienced in veterinary work, was hired to help. Her personal goal was to build a team of dogs, so she saved every penny she could. Within a few months she was able to buy three Alaskan huskies, the foundation for her first team.

In summers Susan worked in a salmon factory on the western coast at the mouth of the Yukon River. Sometimes she lived out of the back of an old Volkswagen, at other times in a tent. As usual, she worked hard at anything she did. Sometimes this disturbed co-workers, who moved at a more relaxed pace. She cut and chopped fish quickly and efficiently, making other employees seem slow. Honest and direct, Susan told them she did not like to talk; she liked to work.

In 1977 the musk-ox project moved to the state's west coast, and Susan followed. Here she met Joe Redington, still enthusiastically training sled dogs at his summer camp. Joe had become well-known for giving help to young mushers. He added more dogs to Susan's team in exchange for her help in training his animals, encouraged her Iditarod dream, and gave her advice on how to prepare.

When Joe returned to his main kennel, still in Knik and one of the largest in the state, Susan worked with his dogs. Joe noticed that she learned quickly, drove herself, and soon was able to do whatever she started better than others. He predicted that some day her dream would come true—she would win the Iditarod.

Alaska suited Susan. At twenty-three years old, she was five feet six inches, compact, and moved with the easy grace of an athlete. Her long brown hair was usually swept out of the way and worn in a braid down her back. Her eyes, blue as her huskies', were clear and direct. Her soft skin glowed with health. Overshadowing all other features was her smile. Wide and dazzling as the northern lights, it transformed her from pretty to beautiful.

Susan continued the pursuit of her dream. In 1977 a bush pilot dropped Susan and her dogs into the wilderness of the southern Wrangell Mountains near the Canadian border. This would be her home base for several years. The remote spot that she chose was known as a "fly in" because the only way in or out of camp was by plane or snowshoe. And the closest civilization was nearly fifty miles away.

She had a gun, tools, and a supply of basic rations for herself and the dogs, including a slab of bacon, a sack of flour, rice, and lots of peanut butter. During hunting seasons, she killed moose, caribou, sheep, and small animals for meat. She chopped firewood and little by little built a cabin. Often she did not see another person for months. That was just what she wanted. In the Alaskan wilderness the young woman from Massachusetts had finally found the space she sought. Here was the spice of danger, the pull of adventure, and the satisfaction of existing by herself. Now it was time to train for the Iditarod.

5

Susan in Training

Athletes preparing for the Olympics and other top sporting events generally have a coach and a gymnasium or a manicured track for practice. Susan had no coach except herself. Her gymnasium was the snow-covered mountains of eastern Alaska. In common with other fine athletes, however, she had the ability to focus on a goal. And she had an unshakable determination to win.

Susan began to build physical stamina in the mountains. Becoming a first-rate musher requires time and patience. It also requires concentration. An Olympic downhill skier stands at the top of the slope, narrows his or her focus to the trail ahead, takes a deep breath, and finally pushes off. The skier's run will be over in two minutes. The Iditarod, however, requires two weeks of total concentration and effort.

Day after day Susan worked with her dogs. They learned to take her commands. Modern racers no longer consider "Mush" a favorite signal for "go" because the sound is too soft. Susan called an encouraging "Hike" or "All right" for "go," "Gee" for "turn right," and

"Haw" for "turn left." Once on the trail, she learned how to direct the dogs' eagerness and high spirits into a steady lope and watch them carefully for signs of dehydration or sprains. She got to know each one's problems or special ways, and which one did not get along with another. In the long days alone on the mountain and away from the distractions of city life, Susan began to enjoy the rhythm of the trail.

Once she discovered the strengths and weaknesses of her dogs, she experimented to find the best leader. The lead dog, intelligent, willing, and confident, is the brains of the team. Incredibly, the rest of the dogs know this and follow without fuss. Even if there are two dogs harnessed in the lead position, one will get across the message, "I am in charge here."

Behind the lead dogs are the "swing" dogs. It is their job to keep the team and the sled on the trail at corners. They help navigate a turn. "Wheel" dogs are exceptionally strong and steady. They are positioned directly in front of the sled and are the first to feel the pull as it breaks loose from the snow. The constant swish of the sled runners just behind bothers some dogs. A young or nervous dog is usually unsuitable in the wheel position.

In Alaska the other dogs between the swing dogs and the wheel dogs are called team dogs. They are chosen for their strength and endurance. The number of dogs in a team varies according to the occasion.

Harnesses, once all leather, are now made of strong, lightweight synthetic materials. The straps over

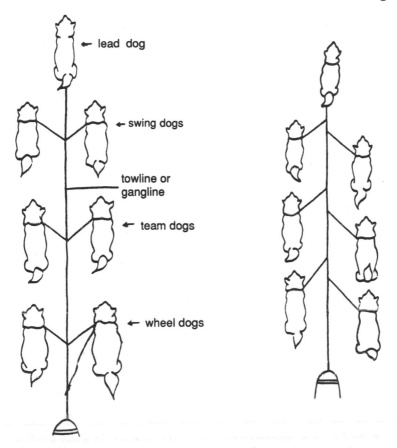

An overview of a dog team labeled with the names for each position. The complicated harnesses ensure that dogs are comfortable as they pull with the shoulder and back muscles, rather than with those of the head and neck.

the back are padded and fitted so that the dog is pulling with the shoulder and back, not the neck and head. Once on the move, a team can run effortlessly for miles.

Depending on the number of dogs in the team, the distance from the sled forward to the lead dog can be more than forty feet. There are no reins, and the musher controls the team by voice commands. On rare occasions a driver will carry a whip, but it never touches the dogs and is only cracked in the air to encourage them to pick up the pace. Most modern mushers have such an affinity with their dogs that the animals will obey without physical prods.

Racing sleds are lightweight and made of wood — ash, birch, and maple are popular choices. The front of the sled curves up and protects the main body of the sled, much like the bumper of a car. In the rear, the sled curves back and up to form a handlebar, which the musher grasps. The sled parts are fastened with thongs for flexibility.

Sled runners are fixed, not movable as they are on

A dogsled team on a mountain trail similar to the ones blazed by Susan Butcher when she lived and trained in the wilderness of the Wrangell Mountains of southeastern Alaska. These dogs are hitched in single file; Susan's are usually hitched with two dogs running side by side. SOURCE: THE LIBRARY OF CONGRESS a downhill sled. Mushers stand on the runners and pedal with one foot to help the sled move faster. This must be timed carefully to synchronize with the dogs' pace or it will jerk the sled and throw the team off stride. Besides the claw foot-brake which slows the team, there is also a snow hook which can be driven into the ground or tied to a tree once the dogs come to a full stop.

The body of the sled is called the "basket." Supplies are loaded into the basket; tired or injured dogs rest there; and sometimes an exhausted musher naps on top of the equipment.

In the mountains Susan chose her first leader, Tekla. She was trail boss over fourteen other dogs, some male and others female. The gender of the dog did not matter to Susan—only what was inside its head and heart. As they traveled each day over the trails, Tekla learned from Susan. It often seemed that the dog was reading her mind. And Susan learned from her as well.

One day they were traveling along the bank of a river, high over the water. The team was moving fast and approaching a left-hand turn.

"Haw!" called Susan.

But Tekla would not turn left. This surprised Susan because the dog had never before refused a command. She called again for a left turn. Instead Tekla swung right off the trail and the team followed. Just as Susan and the sled also made the turn, the snow-covered trail behind collapsed into the river. Had they made the left turn, they would all have crashed into the river and probably drowned.

Tekla knew things about nature that Susan was still learning. During winter months on the trail they met caribou, moose, and wolves. Again Tekla guided them smoothly past potential dangers.

In summer months Susan returned to civilization to earn money, frequently at a fish cannery. That money would be stretched to cover supplies for the next winter. She often supplemented her food rations with moose meat. But one year during the hunting season, she did not get a moose. So she used some of the dogs' food, spiced it up with a few herbs, and added it to a plate of rice for her own "gourmet" dinner.

By 1978 Susan felt they were ready to go for the Iditarod and came back to Knik to prepare. Again Joe Redington helped by finding a sponsor to defray some of the costs of the race. He persuaded a television station to film Susan, clad in a swimsuit, leaping into a hole cut into a frozen pond for a winter ice bath. It was something Susan did frequently, but the publicity drew her first sponsor.

The Iditarod entrance fee was more than $1,000, and there were supplies and food to buy, veterinarians to see, sled and racing gear to find. By February Susan was busy filling burlap sacks with extra food, batteries for her headlamp, hundreds of dog booties, and treats for the dogs and herself. The bags, clearly marked "BUTCHER," would be flown into checkpoints to be picked up when she arrived.

From the beginning, the Iditarod offered an equal arena for both men and women. The rules were exactly the same for all entrants: the mileage between check-points, the number of dogs, the hours of required rest. By 1974, its second year, two women, Mary Shields and Lolly Medley, entered the Iditarod and finished. In 1977 Verona Thompson became the third woman to finish. Starting in the 1978 race were Verona Thompson, Shelly Gill, and Susan Butcher.

Susan was considered a rookie in this race. A rookie is one who has not finished an Iditarod, but who has completed a two-hundred-mile race or run other distances approved by the Trail Committee. At the starting line Susan was so nervous and distracted that she did not even hear the crowd. All her attention was focused on keeping her team together and getting them out on the trail. Once the dogs were away from the excitement and moving smoothly, she began to calm. Tekla, an old friend, was leading the way.

In these early years of the Iditarod, there was time to sit around the campfire at a checkpoint, drink hot coffee, and exchange trail stories with other mushers. Although the race was as tough as everyone promised, Susan had many pleasant hours on the trail. In the mountains there was the peace of a moonlit drive over fresh snow with no sounds but the breathing of the dogs, the swish of sled runners, and the rustle of a light wind. The dogs, tails floating out behind them, ran steadily through the night.

As a rookie, Susan did unusually well in her first race. This year the top twenty mushers received cash prizes, the others received praise, and the last musher won the Red Lantern Award for sweeping the trail clear. Dick Mackey won the race in just under fifteen days and earned the $12,000 first prize. Susan finished in nineteenth place and won a cash award. She was the first woman to finish in the top twenty.

The next year Susan and her team were familiar with the trail and prepared for difficulties. When they pulled into a checkpoint, there was frequently a huge campfire roaring its welcome. After checking in, Susan looked for a quiet place to tie her team. She spread spruce boughs on the ground as comfortable beds for them. Then she collected her sack of supplies, which had arrived by plane, and pulled her gear out of the sled.

She filled a pan with snow and put it on the fire.

An early musher gazes at distant Mount McKinley (Denali), the highest mountain in North America. In 1979, shortly after running her second Iditarod Race, Susan and Joe Redington became the first to take a sled-dog team to its peak, over 20,000 feet high. They spent forty-four days making the trip. SOURCE: THE LIBRARY OF CONGRESS

As it melted, she massaged the dogs' shoulders, rubbed their legs, and tended their paws. She gave them a long drink and mixed dog food into the rest of the water. Once the dogs were fed and curled on the fresh-cut boughs to sleep, Susan ate her own meal. Then she checked equipment, made minor repairs on the sled, repacked, and finally lay down for a brief rest.

Susan had predicted that she would finish in the top ten racers this year. She reached Nome in ninth place. In 1980 she intended to be in the top five, and she finished smoothly in fifth place.

Later that year a young man, David Monson, met

Susan Butcher having fun at New York City's Rockefeller Plaza. New York is one of Susan's favorite cities to visit. She has the freedom here to go anywhere at any time, day or night, much like the freedom she enjoys in Alaska. SOURCE: AP/WIDE WORLD PHOTO

57

Susan when he was selling dog food part-time near her camp. Susan, who thought she had a sponsor committed for the next race, ordered several hundred dollars' worth of food and charged it to the sponsor. The sponsorship plan did not materialize, however, and Susan took over the debt. She did not have enough for the entire bill but paid small amounts regularly. David, accustomed to bad debts, found Susan's honesty refreshing and continued to visit her.

Susan and David had much in common. David, an attorney, had come to Alaska looking for a life that was free of stifling conventions. He had attended college in Colorado. He had also studied in Minnesota, Heidelberg, Germany, and the University of South Dakota, where he received his law degree. Both wished to be judged by what they accomplished, not by their family's pedigrees.

David was good-humored and had a sharp wit that drew out Susan's own sense of fun. He, too, wanted to race sled dogs. When Susan moved permanently to a forested area near Eureka, they continued a long-distance friendship.

6

One, Two, Three

Each race has its memorable moments for Susan. In 1983, she lost nearly an entire day following a mismarked trail. In 1984 near Unalakleet she began the trip over the frozen Norton Sound with Granite leading her team. They were negotiating ice mounds that were often ten feet tall. As the team pulled up the mound, Susan pushed the sled to the top, then held it back on the descent so it would not crush the dogs.

Suddenly the ice began to undulate. It rolled upward and then fell apart when it dropped. Susan and the sled fell into the frigid water below. Her heavy outerwear weighed her down. Granite managed to get to shore and pulled Susan and the team out of danger. Susan's clothes were soaked, and the fur ruff around her face had already stiffened with ice. One way to dry her clothes was to run behind the team. But if she did that too long and gulped in a lot of cold air, her lungs could freeze. If she stood or knelt on the back of the sled, the clothes would not dry and *she* could freeze. She decided to do both; she ran for a while, then rode. In spite of the icy bath, Susan pulled into Nome in second place, just an hour and a half behind Dean Osmar.

By 1985 Susan had become a regular in the Iditarod lineup. She had stayed in the top twenty and had placed second in two previous races. This year her team looked strong. She had raised and trained most of the dogs and spent several years bringing them to top racing condition. Granite would lead. Susan now had a

When deep snow covers the hillsides and valleys in the Alaskan interior, moose and other animals have a difficult time finding food. It is even harder for them to move across normal grazing areas. When they find a cleared path like the Iditarod, it is easier to walk on it than to plow through drifts. Many mushers have met moose on the trail, and they cause no trouble. But in 1985 Susan encountered a pregnant moose, crazed with hunger, which charged into her team. It killed two of the dogs and injured eleven others. Susan withdrew from the race; it was the only year she did not get to Nome. SOURCE: U.S. FISH & WILDLIFE; LIBRARY OF CONGRESS thorough knowledge of the race trails and was in top condition herself. Many veteran mushers thought that 1985 could be her year to win.

The race started well for Susan. As night on the trail approached, she was far ahead of sixty other teams and driving seventeen dogs toward Rabbit Lake. Then as her dogs started up a small hill, she saw the ears of her leaders go up. Susan, forty feet behind the leaders, was driving by now with her headlamp on. She peered through the darkness to see what had disturbed the dogs. Then she came over the hill.

Next to the trail was a huge pregnant moose.

Immediately Susan threw over her sled to stop the dogs. But she wasn't fast enough. The moose, crazed with hunger, was in the middle of the team, stamping and kicking the dogs. Susan grabbed her ax and ran to help them. She waved the ax; she shouted; she poked the huge animal. Nothing stopped the attack.

The dogs were in harness, so they could not get away. Granite went after the attacker, but the moose grabbed him and slammed him into a tree. For twenty minutes the starving moose continued to slash and stomp the team.

Then another musher, Dewey Halverson, came along the trail. He had a gun and shot twice at the moose. After two more shots, the moose finally collapsed. The toll on Susan's team was terrible. One dog was dead, another dying, some had concussions, and several others were badly injured. In all, thirteen of the seventeen dogs had been mauled.

Susan got her dogs to the next checkpoint and assessed her situation. Enough of the dogs were well enough to legally continue the race, but she felt the strain would be too much for her reduced team. She could not ask that of them. She withdrew from the race and flew back to Anchorage with her sick dogs.

Susan stayed in Anchorage with the injured animals. Some required surgery. She slept on the floor of the veterinarian's office several nights to be near them. These were the dogs she had raised and trained, many from the time they were born. Her sense of loss was immeasurable.

Meanwhile the race continued, and it fulfilled predictions that it would be won by a woman. Libby Riddles of Teller, Alaska, was racing a strong team. Near the end of the race, she left a checkpoint in a fearful storm, while the others waited it out. She crossed the finish line in Nome as the first woman to win the Iditarod.

Although 1985 started badly for Susan, it had a happy ending. In late summer of that year, she married her longtime friend David Monson. It was an exuberant wedding, held in the dog yard at her home in Eureka. Susan had flowers braided in her hair and wore a long white gown. David composed a funny, loving poem to read to his new wife. Rick Swenson was a "bridesmaid," and his wife, Cathy, baked a tiered wedding cake. Granite and Tekla were ring bearers.

The cake was cut, and the bridal couple fed each other the first slices. There were toasts, laughter, singing, and dancing. Charlie was on hand with a special gift, a set of encyclopedias to enjoy during winter months. Susan had found the one thing she had been missing in Alaska, a family life with a companion who shared her love of animals and nature.

In the fall, with characteristic single-mindedness, Susan began to rebuild a team for the 1986 Iditarod. The competition would be tough. The team that Libby Riddles ran the year before would be back, driven this time by Libby's partner, Joe Garnie. Rick Swenson, another top musher with four Iditarod wins already, would also be challenging. There were seventy other entrants to consider.

Once again the race started well for Susan. Her new team was pulling hard and responding to her commands. They made the climb up the mountain and through Rainy Pass. Just as they reached a river in the Dalzell Gorge, Susan's leaders disappeared. The rest of the team stopped quickly. Susan moved forward cautiously to see what was wrong.

The two dogs had fallen through the surface ice and were stranded on a second shelf of ice several feet below. As the weather alternately warmed and cooled, an overflow sometimes appeared and refroze, causing a second layer of ice. The hole was too tight to pull the dogs straight up and out. She needed the ax. Susan talked soothingly to the rest of the team. If they decided to move forward, the remaining dogs and the sled would also land in the hole. Chances of the thin ice shelf supporting that extra weight were slim. They could all be killed. She moved back to the sled and stamped the snow hook into the ground. With that anchor in place, she could move more freely. She got the ax, chopped away at the edge of the hole, and called to the dogs. They scrambled upward, and Susan pulled them to safety.

The team continued on for several days, alternating rest and running. As they moved through the Farewell Burn during the night, the teams were stretching out. Susan's team was moving well and soon began to overtake others. When a fast musher approaches a slower team and wishes to pass, the driver calls "Trail." The courtesy of the race requires the slower team to yield. The approaching team moves past on the right. Frequently dogs from each team get tangled with the others. It is especially difficult at night when driving with headlamps. In the bobbing, artificial light, grooves in the trail are hard to see and distances are sometimes distorted.

This year the town of McGrath was the designated halfway point. A prize of several thousand silver dollars is awarded to the first musher to reach the halfway stop. The amount of money varies from year to year but is usually more than $3,000. Joe Garnie was the first into the McGrath checkpoint this year and collected his prize. The very next day he lost the trail and went forty miles out of his way to find it again.

The leaders of the race were beginning to push. At the town of Ruby, Susan was in the lead. Rick Swenson was only a few hours behind. By the tenth day of the

Susan Butcher pulls into the checkpoint at the town of McGrath early in the morning. When the weather is warm, mushers frequently run their teams at night and rest during the day. McGrath, almost halfway into the race, was established in 1907 as a gold-rush town. It was named for an early U.S. marshal, Peter McGrath, and is still a favorite stop along the trail. It has an airfield, restaurants, and sleeping quarters, which make it a popular center for media people who follow the Iditarod race. SOURCE: AP/WIDE WORLD PHOTO

race, it was Susan and Joe Garnie, trading the lead back and forth. By now the drivers were allowing themselves only a few hours of sleep a day. Without enough sleep, mushers frequently get strange hallucinations.

At one point Susan's dogs ran off the trail. Joe's team followed. Susan stopped her sled and walked back to Joe. She waved her arm to the right and told him that they were going to have a terrible time getting back on the trail through all those trees. Actually they were above the Arctic tree line and there wasn't a bit of greenery in sight. When Joe pointed this out, Susan shook her head and laughed. The forest was just a hallucination.

Hallucinations have taken many strange forms in the isolation of the Iditarod. Some mushers have "seen" lights under the feet of the dogs. After many hours on the trail, others have imagined the dogs running up in the air. There has been green grass and pasture seen along the trail. And one musher constantly found a strange man riding in his sled.

The following day word reached Nome that the first musher was on the way in. People dropped everything and ran out into the street to see who this year's winner would be. Bells rang, sirens screamed, and the crowd cheered as Susan Butcher crossed the finish line in first place. Her record-breaking time was eleven days, fifteen hours, and six minutes. Her body was limp with exhaustion, but her smile was wide and warm. She had won the Iditarod!

Susan's prize money looked impressive. It was stacked in a wall of one-dollar bills — 50,000 of them. The people of Nome were churning with excitement for an entire week. It was several days before all the mushers reached Nome. Then the Trail Committee held an awards banquet where all the racers were honored. Each one received a brass buckle and an official Iditarod patch. Susan dressed for the occasion in her special party dress, made from the underwool of the musk-ox.

An honored guest at the banquet was Ed Nollner, the last living musher from the 1925 serum run to Nome. He had waited at Whiskey Creek for the hand-

A patch, similar to this one, is awarded at the postrace banquet to mushers who have completed the race. SOURCE: IDITAROD TRAIL COMMITTEE

over from Bill McCarty and had remained in that area ever since. As the diners applauded the winners, they teased Ed about taking sixty-one years to finally get over the trail and on to Nome.

For Susan it was a week of relaxation and fun. Then it was time to return home and get ready for the next Iditarod. Each year the race has its own risks and twists of fate. Susan always tries to prepare herself for almost any problem. The Iditarod requires the best in physical skills, but good management also plays its part. Good management starts months before the race.

Before each race, Susan, David, and several of their friends get together to prepare the extra food and equipment to fill the bags that are flown into the checkpoints. To be sure that Susan eats properly on the trail, David helps cook her favorite foods, chili rollups and ribs. The dogs burn about eight thousand calories a day

A musher unpacks his sled and prepares to feed his team. Snow is melted on the stove for water and the dogs' stew. If there is a river near the checkpoint, water can be drawn from a hole chopped in the ice.
COURTESY JIM BROWN, IDITAROD TRAIL COMMITTEE

when running, so they mix batches of treats for them, too. Honeyballs are popular with many mushers as special snacks for the team. They are made with ground beef, honey, and vitamins. The food is vacuum-sealed and divided among the storage bags.

To protect dogs' paws on icy trails, mushers carry thousands of dog booties. Susan's friends are particularly helpful in the tedious task of sewing the booties by hand. Most booties are made from polypropylene or fleece, which dry quickly on the trail. They have Velcro tabs to secure them on each foot. If a team has fifteen dogs, that totals sixty paws that must be tended and protected at each checkpoint.

In the 1987 Iditarod lineup, there were at least eight top-notch teams. Each musher and team had its own strengths and game plans. Susan knew it was going to be a tough run.

After starting in good weather, she ran into difficulty for the third year in a row. The first day on the trail, one of her swing dogs, Jackie, suddenly fell over. Susan stopped the team and rushed to her dog. Jackie was not breathing. Susan worked with her, tried mouth-to-mouth resuscitation, but it was no use. Jackie was dead. A later examination showed that the dog had a hereditary liver dysfunction from birth. There was nothing Susan could have done to save her.

There were other kinds of pressure. Rick Swenson, always a tough competitor, was moving fast. Two other top mushers, Austin and Halverson, decided to run together and had set a fast pace from the beginning. They hoped to outdistance the others in the early part of the race and capture a comfortable lead.

This year on the southern leg of the route, the town of Iditarod was the halfway point. Austin was the first musher into the checkpoint. He collected his bowl of silver dollars. Halverson was second into Iditarod, and Susan was just behind in third position.

Over the years a legend had grown about the halfway prize winner. Only once in Iditarod history had that musher gone on to a final victory in Nome. So the superstitious said that anyone who won the silver dollars would not capture first place in the race.

Ninety miles past Iditarod the southern trail reaches the Yukon River and turns north. In clear weather, the frozen riverbed is like a highway. Susan encouraged her dogs to pick up speed, and the team skimmed along the trail. At Kaltag, just before the swing to the coast, the teams of Austin and Halverson began to tire. By the time the race reached Unalakleet and the coast, Susan was out in front.

But now Rick Swenson was moving up. The two teams were close together as they pushed north past the frozen Norton Sound. Then at the Elim checkpoint, Rick's dogs began to drop back. On the final stretch along the coast, Susan pulled away.

Her dogs still had plenty of stamina, but she began to run up every hill to ease the strain on them. This was no small achievement, for she wore several layers of clothing, heavy boots, and a furred hood that partially

Susan Butcher racing down Front Street in Nome on her way to a second consecutive win in the Iditarod Trail Sled Dog Race of 1987. SOURCE: AP/WIDE WORLD PHOTOS

obscured her vision. Driving through mists of falling snow, Susan looked back frequently but could see no pursurer. Rick was still near Elim and would not catch her. Pushing, running, encouraging her dogs, she went for the finish line. She ran up Front Street and arrived thirteen hours ahead of her previous record-setting time. For the second consecutive time, she crossed the finish line in first place.

Granite and Tolstoy were Susan's leaders in the 1988 Iditarod. She trained her dogs to be self-confident, but Granite had been a slow starter. At one time he had been shy and unfocused. Now Susan put her trust in her team, and they, in turn, trusted her. This mutual regard was of significant help in the 1988 race.

Two days into the race they reached the Dalzell

The cabin used by volunteers at the Rohn checkpoint, one of the most peaceful stops in the Iditarod race. At many of the other checkpoints, volunteers use shelters or cabins where the original serum-run mushers waited in 1925. COURTESY JIM BROWN, IDITAROD TRAIL COMMITTEE

Gorge. Susan's sled, which had bounced and bashed against the boulders, needed repair. When they arrived at the Rohn checkpoint, she declared her twenty-four-hour layover, fed the dogs, and bedded them down. Then she spent most of the remaining time repairing her sled.

After Rohn, the trail wound through the dreary Farewell Burn, along the Yukon River, and out to the coast. There was a tremendous storm brewing. Although the weather contributed to an especially beautiful show of northern lights, it was distracting for the sled dogs.

On the tenth day out, Susan was still behind the leaders, as she had been for most of the race. When the storm blew in, many of the others stopped to wait it out. The coast was the most dangerous part of the trail. Even Inuit villagers, whose families had lived in the area for generations and were familiar with dangerous storms, sometimes froze to death if caught in a white-out.

Susan's dogs had been trained in February runs and knew the coast. They always went well in this kind of weather, when other dogs balked and refused to move. She decided to keep going. The wind came in at a slant, strong enough to knock the dogs off their feet and flip over the sled.

Susan stopped repeatedly to wipe the dogs' frozen eyelashes and pat them encouragingly. She tried to kneel on the runners to avoid the wind, but then she could not see ahead to the trail markers. The sled went over several times, and she lost some loose equipment.

They crossed the ridges of pack ice carefully because they were covered with chunks of frozen snow. The only way Susan could tell if they were over the ice and back on land was to dig a hole and look for signs of grass. The team made it safely to shore and then went directly for Nome.

Susan and the team arrived a full fourteen hours ahead of the closest musher. Her bold move out into the storm and her trust in her powerful dogs brought its reward. She became the first ever to win three Iditarod races in a row. Officials now considered her one of the best mushers in the world.

7

Susan at Home

Running the Iditarod is not just a two-week event for Susan Butcher. Following each race, she spends the rest of the year preparing for the next one. Her home is one hundred miles south of the Arctic Circle near Eureka, Alaska. In 1980 she bought the land for its scenery and seclusion. It is frequently reported in Manley, a neighboring town, that there are more dogs than people living in Eureka.

Two of the people are Susan and her husband, David, and almost 150 of the dogs belong to them. Their Trail Breaker Kennels is a five-acre spread in a hilly forest. In a clearing are several cabins and an entire village of doghouses. Visitors, rounding a curve in the road to the kennels, are sometimes startled when they see more than one hundred dogs, each sitting Snoopy-like on its own wooden house or lying in the shade nearby.

Susan's dogs are Alaskan huskies, descended from Indian dogs. "Husky" is a corruption of the Algonquin Indian name for Eskimo, "esky." When Susan began to put together her early teams, she bought good dogs, even going into debt to get the best. The huskies, smaller than malamutes, are lean and bred for speed and endurance. Their average weight is fifty pounds. They are not a registered American Kennel Association breed, but that does not matter to the many people who want to buy Trail Breaker dogs. They sell at anywhere from $1,000 to $10,000 apiece. Mushers and other breeders are frequent buyers, and many of the dogs become part of Iditarod teams.

Show dogs are usually judged by their size and handsome features. It is not important to Susan what a dog looks like on the outside. She cares about what is inside. Does this dog have the heart and intelligence to be a good trail dog? Does it have the confidence to lead a team across an ice bridge in freezing weather? Does it have a true desire to run?

Taking care of one hundred dogs and fifty puppies entirely fills Susan's days. She and David are always up early, usually by 5:30 A.M. There is no running water in their cabin, so they haul all their water from a nearby creek. In the morning the dogs get a special broth of ground beef, vitamins, and dry dog food mixed with water. It is the first feeding of the day and takes several hours to distribute a portion to each dog.

After the dogs are cared for, Susan spends time on her own conditioning. Sometimes she works out on a rowing machine; sometimes she runs through the forest. There are more than two hundred miles of trail for her to use. Then she has breakfast, does a few inside chores, and is back outside with the dogs.

Susan begins handling the new puppies as soon as they are born. When they are a few days old, she picks them up, pets them, talks softly to them. Gently she blows in their faces. This helps the puppy recognize the human scent and look forward to the arrival of this good person.

When the puppies are ready to leave their mothers, they move into the puppy pen and begin socializing with others. Susan pays daily visits, and the puppies recognize her when she comes into the pen. She sits down and holds out her arms. They come in a rush, tails wagging like windup toys. They scramble over one another, wriggling under Susan's arms, licking her face, trying to snatch off her hat.

When the puppies are about two months old, she takes them, a few at a time, on walks. They go through creeks, over rocks, into wooded areas. Susan watches each puppy to see which is eager to climb over the rocks, investigate logs, or show curiosity about the bottom of the creek bed. She wants them to eventually care about what is around the next corner.

Next she tries the young dogs on the circular dog walker. Each dog is hooked to an overhead wheel and walks in circles for a half hour. Susan watches the speed and gait of each dog. Both these factors are important when choosing a team for the Iditarod.

In August when the first cool temperatures arrive, serious training begins. The dogs sense the excitement as harnesses and gear come out of storage. Since there is little or no snow on the ground at this time of year,

Susan Butcher playing with one of her Trail Blazer Kennel puppies. She raises and trains approximately fifty young dogs and one hundred mature ones each season. Her dogs are bred for speed and endurance, and are trained with a mixture of affection, sound diets, and discipline. SOURCE: PRO-VISION PET SPECIALTY ENTERPRISES

Susan harnesses a team to an ATV, climbs into the seat, and calls to the dogs. They can hardly wait to get out on the trail.

Susan and David begin taking the teams out

around noon. The trips are short at first but get longer as the dogs gain endurance. An experienced dog is generally harnessed with a rookie. They run through the nearby forests, using different trails to keep the dogs from getting bored. By December, they're running from twenty-five to seventy-five miles a day. Then Susan begins the process of selecting the twenty dogs that seem best qualified for her Iditarod team.

At the end of a long day, Susan frequently soaks her aches away in a wooden tub, her "spa," outside the cabin. Each evening she and David bring several dogs inside for extra attention. She feels this has been helpful in making her dogs willing leaders. Besides, she loves playing with them, even though it means covering the furniture and sharing space.

Susan is so in tune with the animals that she can recognize each voice and every different howl. Her huskies have a different sound for nearly every occasion. Although they may just sound like barking dogs to others, to Susan, they are communicating the news that someone is coming, or the weather is going to change, or they are happy, or they want companionship.

The main cabin on the property measures approximately fifteen by twenty feet. It was once a blacksmith's shop that served people at a nearby gold-mining site. It is called an "inside-out" cabin, because the former owner got tired of looking at walls blackened by smoke, so he dismantled the cabin and rebuilt it with the dark side turned out and the weathered one on the inside. Susan and David sleep in this cabin. Another cabin is for cooking and bookwork. Others are used as storage for equipment, dog food, and a generator.

Their land is more than one hundred miles from Fairbanks, where the closest veterinarian lives. Because of this isolation, Susan's experiences as a veterinarian's assistant has been invaluable. She can give shots, check heart rates, and even deliver newborn puppies. David handles the generator, which keeps light and heat available, and deals with mountains of paperwork.

Susan and David enter other races, both in Alaska and in the lower forty-eight states. In 1986, the first year that she won the Iditarod, Susan logged more than 2,600 racing miles—more than any other racer in history. David won the prestigious Yukon Quest race one year and was in second place another year. In many others Susan set new speed records. Among the races are the Coldfoot 350—north of the Arctic Circle; the Norton Sound 250; the Kusko 300; the Kobuk 220 and 440; the John Beargrease (Minnesota); and the Copper Basin.

The prize money from these races is put to instant use. The dogs at Trail Breaker eat about 250 pounds of dog food every day. They drink one hundred gallons of water. There must be money for clothes, medicine for the dogs, lots of straw, and entrance fees for the races.

Susan is a celebrity in the sports world. Fame carries responsibilities. Although she would prefer to spend her summers with David and the dogs in the forest, she sets aside time for public appearances. She has visited hospitals, spoken on behalf of the American Cancer Society's no-smoking campaign, and been a gracious guest at interviews, dinners, and award ceremonies. Several sponsors have helped her, and she visits them as well during the summer, signing autographs and posing for photographs.

To look at the photos, one would never think that Susan could put in a day at the kennels that would grind most people to powder. But she obviously loves what she does. She has the attractive glow of an outdoor person. Her movements are fluid, but economical, and there is no time wasted when she works. Although she initially can be distant with strangers, she is animated and loving when caring for her dogs, and exuberant and full of fun with David and their friends. She delights in giving gag gifts to her husband and wrapped Christmas presents to all the dogs.

While others have grown to expect a good performance from Susan, she expects even more of herself. She is continually responding to her own inner pressure and has the one indispensable quality of a champion — drive.

8

Breaking Records

For Susan, there is always another hill to climb, another race to run. The 1988 Iditarod made her the race's top record breaker, earning an unprecedented three victories in succession.

Although the 1989 Iditarod had only forty-nine entrants, the lowest number in many years, the regular top racers were back. The weather, as usual, played an important part in shaping the race. This year there was heavy snow, though the days were mild. During the day the trails turned to slush, so many mushers rested during the day and traveled at night when the temperatures dropped.

The trail through Farewell Burn, normally tedious and grim, was transformed by the deep snow into a highway. Several days into the race Jerry Austin, a veteran musher, and four rookies found an unconscious racer by the side of the trail. They worked with the young man, packed him in blankets, got him to a checkpoint and onto a plane back to Nome. Then Jerry returned to get the man's team. He lost eighteen hours, but the patient recovered. The Iditarod Trail Committee later gave all five rescuers sportsmanship awards.

That year the halfway point was set at Iditarod. As racers neared the ghost town, Joe Runyan was in the lead. Although Susan had been having trouble with sick dogs, she was close behind Joe, and she knew this part of the trail well. Her team passed Joe's in the dark and arrived first at the Iditarod checkpoint. It was her turn to win the halfway prize. Officials congratulated her and poured $3,000 in silver coins into a large bowl. This was the lucky part of the stop.

Not so lucky was the trail virus picked up by her dogs, who were not responding to the veterinarians' medicines. She had managed to have straw flown into Iditarod in advance. She broke up the bales and spread straw along the ground. The weakened dogs rested comfortably on the padding of fresh straw.

After the rest, the veterinarian examined Susan's dogs and Joe's too. He ruled that both teams were fit to continue. After this long break, Susan started back on the trail. Joe was already far ahead.

Joe had come to Alaska in 1971 to fight forest fires. Through the years he built a kennel of fine dogs. Like many of the other top mushers, Joe was a planner. He worked out mileage, rest stops, food amounts, and countless details ahead of the race. They were recorded in a notebook, which he consulted regularly.

By the time Joe reached Kaltag, Susan was just behind him. Surprisingly, when they got to the coast at Unalakleet, there was no wind. Again Joe pulled ahead, ran hard on the last stretch of trail, and reached Nome as the 1989 Iditarod winner. Susan crossed the finish line an hour later for second place. Her team held together. She was pleased with them and took her defeat graciously. There would be another year.

The Iditarod is never a dull competition. In 1990 the weather in Anchorage was almost too warm for comfortable racing. And there had been a five-foot snowfall, which drew moose onto the trail in search of food.

Newly arrived from Eureka, Susan calmly washed her hair at the hotel. Joe Runyan was here with a strong team. Rick Swenson was ready to go. Dee Dee Jonrowe and other top mushers were making their preparations. A little snow was not going to stop them.

The race started as usual through the streets of Anchorage, then wound out onto the trail. The soft snow made traveling slow, and the officials were not expecting any record-breaking runs this race. In spite of the unusual number of foraging moose, Susan did not meet one this year. She met a buffalo instead.

She came up the trail to find Tim Osmar and his team blocked by a large buffalo, which stood right in the middle of the trail. There was plenty of noise. The dogs were barking, Tim was yelling and firing his gun in the air. But the buffalo stood firm. As Susan came closer, the animal noticed her red racing suit, which seemed to rattle him. Susan, waving her red-clad arms and shouting, joined forces with Tim. Finally the buffalo stumbled off the trail, and the race continued.

The deep snow made a welcome cushion on the challenging ridges of the Happy River ascent. Farther into the interior, mushers faced an unusual problem. Redoubt Volcano, two hundred miles away and inactive for twenty-five years, erupted. Most of the leaders escaped its effect, but those traveling farther back were caught in the fallout. The air swirled with volcanic ash. It stung everyone's eyes and noses, made breathing difficult, and left a terrible taste in their mouths. The gritty ash was so thick that in some cases, mushers could not even see their lead dogs.

In addition to buffalo, there were many moose foraging near the trail. Several racers encountered them. One put on his snowshoes and led his team around the moose. Another musher startled a moose, and it bolted off the trail. Rick Swenson met one near the halfway point. The moose charged past his leaders, but hit some of the dogs in midteam. Damage was not severe, but one dog was left with an injured jaw, and Rick was delayed for some time.

In 1990 the Iditarod took the northern route, and Cripple was the halfway checkpoint. Lavon Barve of Wasilla was in first and collected the $3,000 prize in silver dollars. Later Susan pulled into the lead and was the first into the Yukon River checkpoint, Ruby. Here she found another sort of prize. The chef and several waiters from an Anchorage hotel had flown in a seven-course dinner to treat the first musher to arrive at the Yukon. Susan fed and checked her dogs and then went into the cabin to eat. There was candlelight, music, good

Susan Butcher dining in style in the wilderness at Ruby. In 1990, the first musher to reach this outpost on the Yukon River was greeted by the chef of an Anchorage hotel and served an elegant meal. Susan enjoys the food as her fans stand by and relish every bite. No detail was overlooked by the hotel; even the bread basket is shaped like a sled. SOURCE: AP/WIDE WORLD PHOTO

china, elegant food—all unexpected in such wilderness. As Susan picked up her fork, she wondered aloud when she had last eaten. Everyone in the cabin was able to tell her. She had not had any food since the checkpoint at Ophir. They had all been following the race on the radio. Susan nodded; she understood.

Susan is a favorite with the ham radio operators. She is usually one of the racers out in front and breaking trail. When asked, she will pick up the microphone at a checkpoint and report detailed information for the less experienced rookies. She will tell where the trail is soft, which is the best area to find shelter, how strong the wind is blowing. Not many of the competitors are so willing to share information.

She left Ruby, pushed on to Nulato, and turned south on the Yukon River. Moonlight shone on the glistening ice. The dogs moved silently and swiftly. The beauty and tranquillity of these special times when Susan and her team work as a unit to reach a challenging goal are magnets that draw her again and again to the Iditarod.

Lavon Barve was first to reach the coast and Unalakleet. Susan and Joe Runyan followed an hour later. After resting and caring for the dogs, all three pushed north again. By the Shaktoolik checkpoint, Susan and Joe caught Barve, and by Koyuk, Susan was ahead of them all by one hour. There was nothing ahead but fresh trail and Nome.

Just before she reached Elim, however, one of her leaders, Longhorn, began to limp. Because of the deep snow early in the race, Susan had dropped two tired leaders, Granite and Mattie. Longhorn was the last of her veterans. She pulled into the checkpoint and searched for the vet. Gently he felt Longhorn's shoulder and leg. It was a sprain, and this dog, too, must be left behind. Susan dropped a kiss on Longhorn's nose, unhooked him, and led him to a quiet place.

Susan had been the first competitor to train her dogs on the coast. Each February she brought them for a winter run along the shore. So, even though she had lost the three leaders who had made the trip over and over, her remaining dogs knew the trail. The February training had been a sensible precaution, but Susan was not sure how the team would respond.

They responded beautifully. After a two-hour rest, they left Elim running strong and steady. Joe Runyan came into Elim and stopped only long enough to sign the checker's record book. Then he called up his dogs and started after Susan.

At White Mountain Susan stopped for the race's second mandatory layover. She took her time feeding the dogs and bedding them down. The village children, slushing along on short skis, followed every move. Susan signed autographs and chatted with her young fans, then went inside the checkpoint cabin to rest.

On the last day of the race, Susan was running

Each year the schoolchildren of Alaska are invited to design a booster button for the next year's Iditarod and receive an award. The 1992 entry marked the twentieth running of the Last Great Race and was designed by twelve-year-old Marvin Captain, a sixth-grade student from Ruby.
SOURCE: IDITAROD TRAIL COMMITTEE

steadily for Nome. She knew Joe Runyan was on her heels and looked back frequently. She did not see him, because he was two hours behind her. Susan and her young team sped into Nome and across the finish line. It hardly seemed possible to her that she had become a four-time champion of the toughest race in the world. Her record time was eleven days, one hour, fifty-three minutes, and twenty-three seconds.

Susan, as usual, stopped to pat her dogs. Then she found David, got a giant hug, and moved to the winners' podium. With two of her leaders, she sat under the arch and smiled as wreaths of yellow flowers were placed around their necks. Since 1973, when she first read about the Iditarod, this was the dream she had pursued.

Susan Butcher was the most famous dogsled musher in the world.

In 1987 Susan Butcher shares the spotlight under the arch in Nome with two special friends, her lead dogs. Mattie is on the left, Granite on the right. Source: AP/Wide World Photo

A frosted Susan Butcher coming into Nome to claim her fourth Iditarod victory and a new speed record in 1990. SOURCE: AP/WIDE WORLD PHOTO

Susan rounded out fifteen years on the Iditarod by placing third in 1991 and second in 1992. In both of those years, she pulled back to spare her team. Weather was a key factor again. One of the worst blizzards in Iditarod history hit the coast in 1991. Susan was in the lead but turned back when her dogs went into a dense "wall" of wind and snow. In 1992 the weather was cold and dry, making trail conditions fast, and generating a record-breaking pace. Susan was behind the leader but pulled off to rest her dogs.

After her first rookie race, Susan had placed every year in the top ten mushers. In eleven of those years she was in the top five, and in four of them she was first. It was a record that won respect throughout the world of sports and secured her place in history as a top Iditarod champion.

Through the years, many have heard and answered Alaska's "call of the wild." Susan had felt that call since she was a child, and its voice strengthened gradually over a period of years. Once she thought she had been born in the wrong place and in the wrong century. But it is now clear that she is exactly where she should be. Honest, direct, hardworking, and full of humor, she has become a role model for a whole generation of young people.

In her future, Susan hopes to start a family, establish an animal research area, and enjoy the beauty of her wilderness home. Whatever waits on the trail ahead, she will meet it with energy, resolve, and success.

Iditarod Routes

NORTHERN ROUTE

(Even-numbered years)

CHECKPOINT	MILES
Anchorage to Eagle River	20
Eagle River to Wasilla	29
Wasilla to Knik	14
Knik to Skwentna	88
Skwentna to Finger Lake	45
Finger Lake to Rainy Pass	30
Rainy Pass to Rohn	48
Rohn to Nikolai	93
Nikolai to McGrath	48
McGrath to Takotna	23
Takotna to Ophir	38
Ophir to Cripple	60
Cripple to Sulatna Crossing	45
Sulatna Crossing to Ruby	75
Ruby to Galena	52
Galena to Nulato	52
Nulato to Kaltag	42

CHECKPOINT	MILES
Kaltag to Unalakleet	90
Unalakleet to Shaktoolik	40
Shaktoolik to Koyuk	58
Koyuk to Elim	48
Elim to Golovin	28
Golovin to White Mountain	18
White Mountain to Safety	55
Safety to Nome	22
Total	1,161

SOUTHERN ROUTE

(Odd-numbered years)

CHECKPOINT	MILES
Anchorage to Eagle River	20
Eagle River to Wasilla	29
Wasilla to Knik	14
Knik to Skwentna	88
Skwentna to Finger Lake	45
Finger Lake to Rainy Pass	30
Rainy Pass to Rohn	48*
Rohn to Nikolai	93
Nikolai to McGrath	48
McGrath to Takotna	23
Takotna to Ophir	38

*SOURCE: IDITAROD TRAIL COMMITTEE

CHECKPOINT	MILES
Ophir to Iditarod	90
Iditarod to Shageluk	65
Shageluk to Anvik	25
Anvik to Grayling	18
Grayling to Eagle Island	60*
Eagle Island to Kaltag	70
Kaltag to Unalakleet	90
Unalakleet to Shaktoolik	40*
Shaktoolik to Koyuk	58
Koyuk to Elim	48
Elim to Golovin	28
Golovin to White Mountain	18
White Mountain to Safety	55
Safety to Nome	22
Total	**1,163**

*SOURCE: IDITAROD TRAIL COMMITTEE

Twenty Years of Iditarod Winners*

1973—92

YEAR	WINNER	DAYS	HRS	MIN	SEC	PRIZE
1973	Dick Wilmarth	20	—	49	41	$12,000
1974	Carl Huntington	20	15	01	07	12,000
1975	Emmitt Peters	14	14	43	15	15,000
1976	Jerry Riley	18	22	58	17	7,200
1977	Rick Swenson	16	16	27	13	9,600
1978	Dick Mackey	14	18	52	24	12,000
1979	Rick Swenson	15	10	37	47	12,000
1980	Joe May	14	07	11	51	12,000
1981	Rick Swenson	12	08	45	02	24,000
1982	Rick Swenson	16	04	40	10	24,000
1983	Dick Mackey	12	14	10	44	24,000
1984	Dean Osmar	12	15	07	33	24,000
1985	Libby Riddles	18	—	20	17	50,000
1986	Susan Butcher	11	15	06	—	50,000
1987	Susan Butcher	11	02	05	13	50,000
1988	Susan Butcher	11	11	41	40	30,000†

*Source: Iditarod Trail Committee
†1988 purse was smaller than usual; the 1st prize was also smaller.

YEAR	WINNER	DAYS	HRS	MIN	SEC	PRIZE
1989	Joe Runyan	11	05	24	34	50,000
1990	Susan Butcher	11	01	53	23	50,000
1991	Rick Swenson	12	16	34	39	50,000
1992	Martin Buser	10	19	17	—	50,000

Susan Butcher, Fifteen Years on the Iditarod Trail

YEAR	FINISHING POSITION*
1978	19
1979	9
1980	5
1981	5
1982	2
1983	9
1984	2
1985	—†
1986	1
1987	1
1988	1
1989	2
1990	1
1991	3
1992	2

*TOP FIVE; ELEVEN TIMES. TOP TEN; THIRTEEN TIMES.
†WITHDREW (MOOSE KILLED DOGS).

Susan Butcher, Awards and Honors

U.S. Sports Academy Female Athlete of the Year (1987)
Professional Athlete of the Year, Women's Sports Foundation
(1987 and 1988)
Victor Award, Female Athlete of the Year (1987 and 1988)
U.S. Academy of Achievement Athlete of the Year (1988)
Sled-Dog Racer of the Decade (Anchorage Times, *1989)*
Tanqueray Athlete of the Year (1989)
Outstanding Female Athlete of the World
(International Academy of Sports in France, 1989)
Top Professional Sportswoman of 1990
*(*USA Today*/U.S. Sports Academy Athlete of the Year)*
Outstanding Achiever (Lab School of Washington, 1991)
Outstanding Young American (U.S. Jaycees, 1991)

Index

Index